The Ultimate Fat Book

Jim Erskine with Bobbi Carby Cooper

The Ultimate Fat Book

Angus & Robertson Publishers

To Bobbi, who is responsible,
And to Marian, who is not.

ANGUS & ROBERTSON PUBLISHERS
London • Sydney • Melbourne

First published in the United States by Holt, Rinehart & Winston 1982
First published in the United Kingdom by Angus & Robertson (UK) Ltd 1983
First published in Australia by Angus & Robertson Publishers, Australia, 1983
Reprinted 1983

ISBN 0 207 14669 1

Printed in Great Britain by
Richard Clay (The Chaucer Press) Ltd, Bungay, Suffolk

DANGER!!
MINE FIELD

SUPER GLUE ALL
SUPER·GLUE

·1 GROSS·
ACME
CARROT
GRATERS
GLUE

PORK
CHOPS 79¢
lb.

GIVE

FREEZER

APE
DRMS

WORK!
WORK!
WORK!

ACME
DIET BELT

PRE
POST

KNOCK
HIS
BLOCK
OFF
3 SWINGS -
25¢

"HOLEY"
GIRDLE
ACME "HOLEY" GIRDLE

LEECHES

THE AMAZING
GAG
O
MATIC

INSTRUCTIONS
① INSERT FINGER INTO

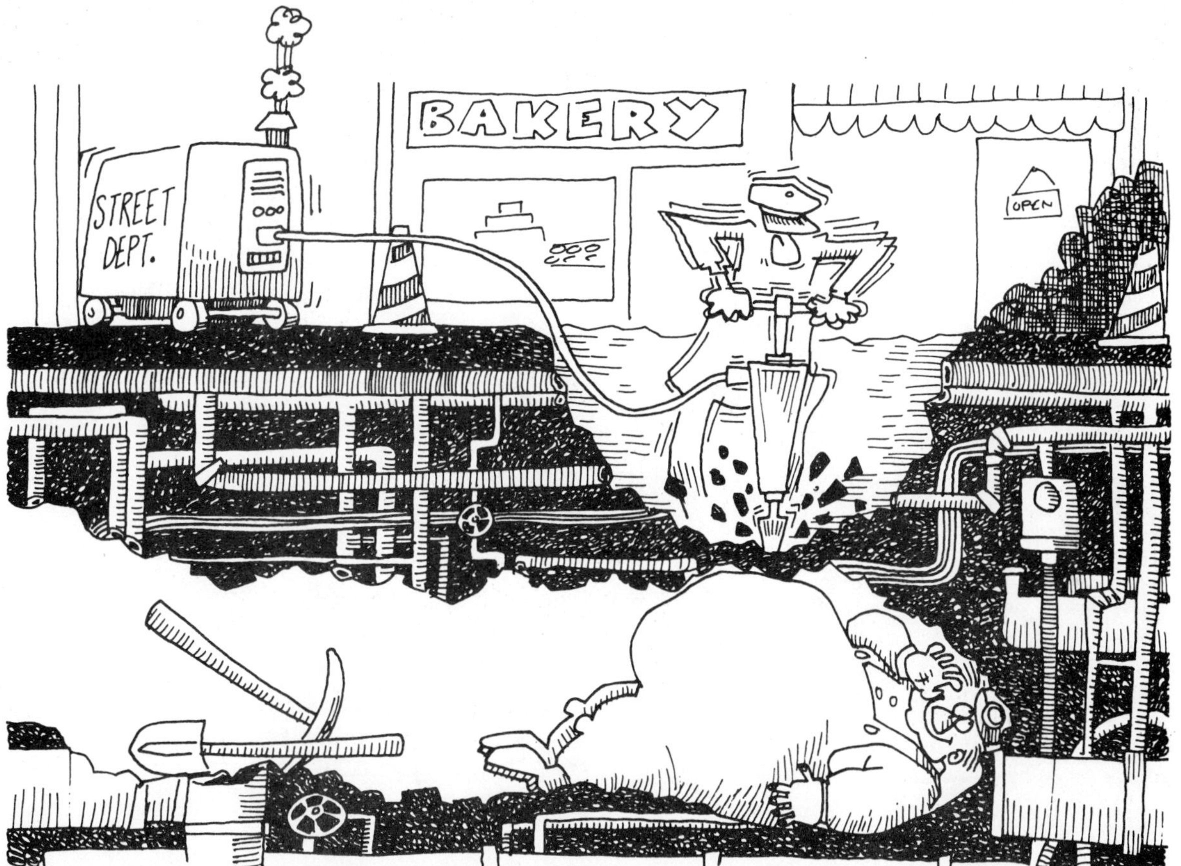

STREET DEPT.
BAKERY
OPEN

DINGA DINGA DINGA

DAD
BB's

AUGUST
DO NOT
OPEN
TIL
XMAS

PIRAHNA
BRAND
DIET
JACUZZI

MR.
BAR·B·Q

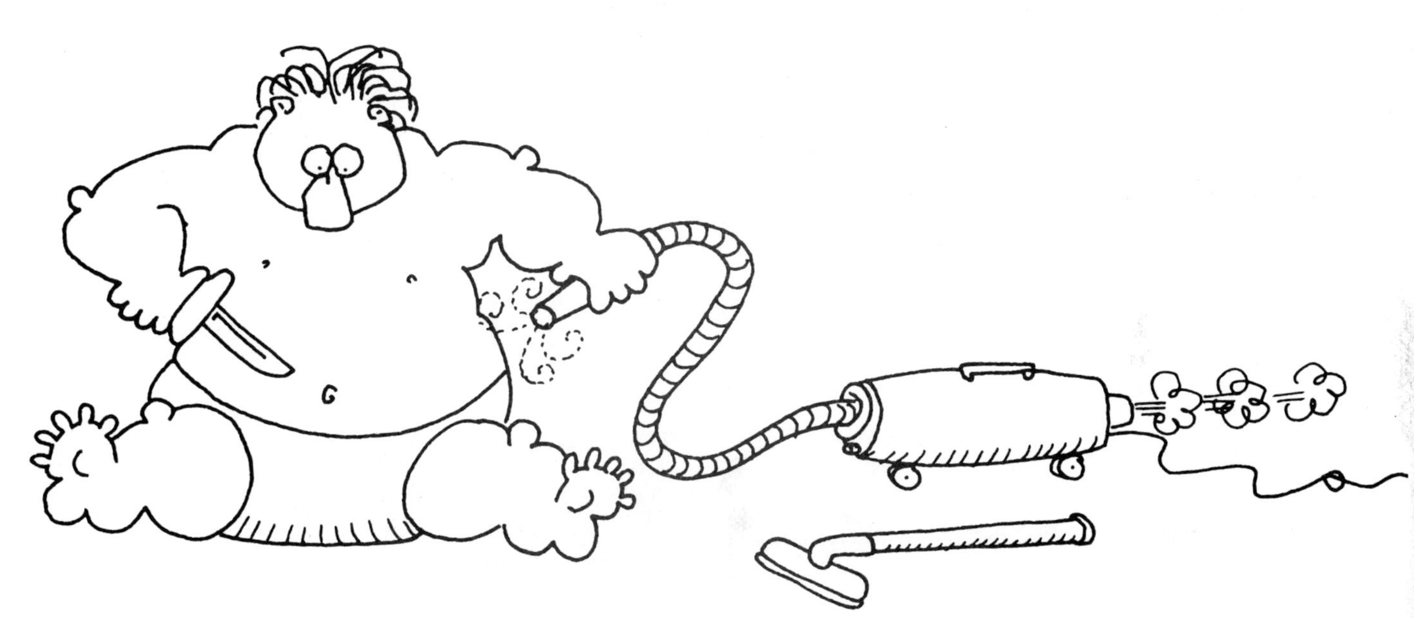

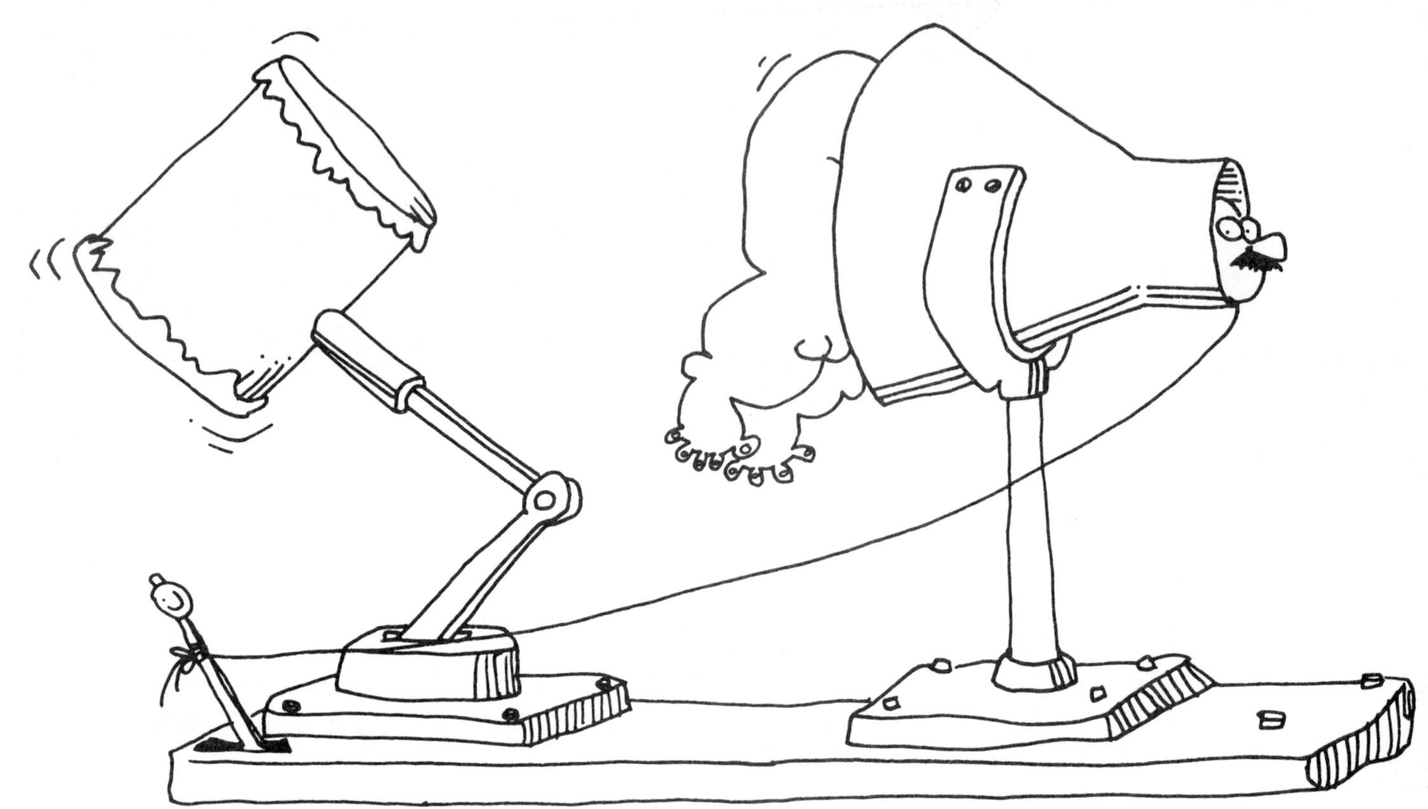

LION

ALUM

HONEY

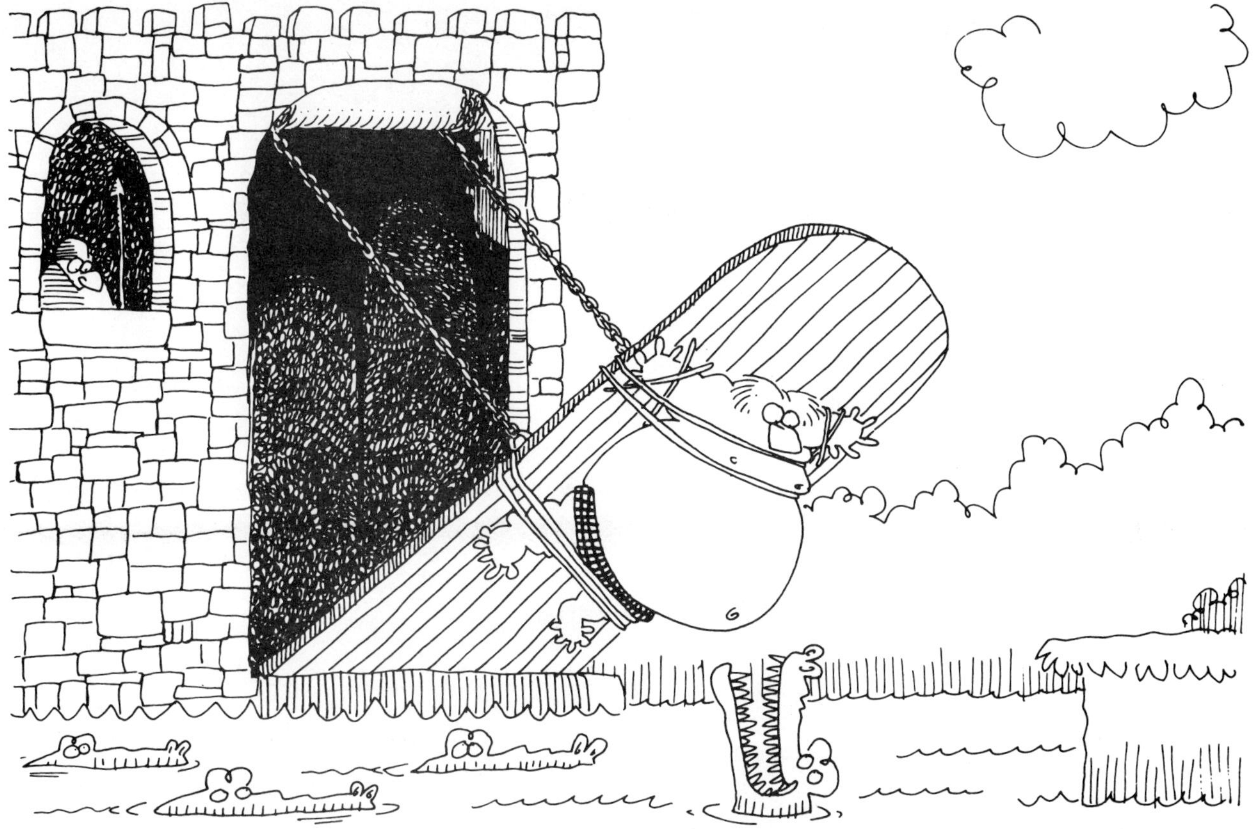

1'
2'
3'
4'
5'
6'
7'
8'

LAXO
CANDY BARS
LAXO
CANDY BARS
LAXO
CANDY BARS
LAXO
CANDY BARS.
LAXO
CANDY BARS
LAXO
CANDY BARS
LAXO
CANDY BARS
LAXO
CANDY BARS
LAXO
CANDY BARS
ZZZZ

DEPOSIT
TRASH
HERE
ON
OFF

RUBBER
BANDS

ACID
ACID
ACID

GAS

· · EAT N' PULL · ·
STOMACH LINERS

VIBRA
MASSAGE
MED
LO HI
OFF ULTRA
HI
25¢

CEMENT

MIAMI
OR
BUST

MIAMI
900 MILES